Hartley
Field

Books by Connie Wanek

Hartley Field (2002)

Bonfire (1997)

Hartley Field

poems by

Connie Wanek

HOLY COW! PRESS · 2002 · DULUTH, MINNESOTA

Library of Congress Cataloging-in-Publication Data

Wanek, Connie, 1952-
    Hartley Field: poems / by Connie Wanek.
      p. cm.
    ISBN 0-930100-99-9
      1. Minnesota—Poetry. I. Title.

PS3573.A47686 H37 2002
811'.54—dc21   2002027318

The author would like to thank the Arrowhead Regional Arts Council for generous
fellowship support during the period when many of these poems were written. She
would also like to thank the Jerome Foundation for a Study and Travel grant.

Grateful acknowledgment is made to the following authors and publishers from
which quotations in this collection were taken: Robert Bly, from *Morning Poems*,
published by HarperCollins Publishers, Inc., in 1997; Tomas Tranströmer, from
Baltics, translated by Samuel Charters, published by Oyez Press in 1975, and *The
Sorrow Gondola*, translated by Robin Fulton, published by The Dedalus Press in
1996; Issa, from T*he Year of My Life*, translated by Nobuyuki Yuasa, published by
the University of California Press in 1972; and T. S. Eliot, *Collected Poems 1909-
1962*, published by Harcourt, Brace and World, Inc. in 1963.

Holy Cow! Press books are distributed to the trade by Consortium Book Sales &
Distribution, 1045 Westgate Drive, Saint Paul, Minnesota 55114. Our books are
also available through all major library distributors and jobbers, and through most
small press distributors, including Bookpeople and Small Press Distribution. For
personal orders or other information, write to: Holy Cow! Press, Post Office Box
3170, Mount Royal Station, Duluth, Minnesota 55803.

Acknowledgments

Grateful acknowledgment is given to the following publications in which poems from this collection first appeared:

Artword Quarterly: "Little Trout" and "Late September"

Briar Cliff Review: "Lemon"

Great River Review: "The Exchange" and "The Yearling"

Minnesota Monthly: "Tag," "Wild Strawberries," and "Swings"

Minnesota Poetry Calendar: "Ladder" and "Summer Night"

North Coast Review: "Honesty"

Poetry: "All Saints' Day," "Butter," "After Us," "Checkers," "Hartley Field," "The Hypnotist," and "Jump Rope"

Prairie Schooner: "Memorial Day at the Lake" and "So Like Her Father"

Quarterly West: "Postcard: Busy Clarence Town Harbor on a Mail Boat Day"

Rhino: "Hard Frost"

River Oak Review: "The Fugitive" and "New Snow"

The Atlantic Monthly: "The Coin Behind Your Ear"

The Talking of Hands: (an anthology from New Rivers Press) "Peaches" and "The Hammer"

The Texas Observer: "Daisies" and "Children Near the Water"

To Topio: "Woman Knitting"

Water-Stone: "Christmas Fable" and "Poodles"

Willow Review: "Horses in Spring," "Grown Children," "An April Walk with My Daughter," and "The Ventriloquist"

"After Us" was chosen by Poet Laureate Billy Collins for the Library of Congress Poetry 180 project for the year 2002.

For my father and mother,
Ralph and Betty Wanek

Table of Contents

Three

One

The Coin Behind Your Ear

Before you knew you owned it
it was gone, stolen, and you were a fool.
How you never felt it is the wonder,
heavy and thick,
lodged deep in your hair like a burr.
You still see the smile of the magician
as he turned the coin in his long fingers
which had so disturbed your ear
with their caress. You watched him
lift it into the light, bright as frost,
and slip it into his maze of pockets.
You felt vainly behind your ear
but there was no second coin,
nothing to tempt him back.
No one cared to know why he did it,
only how.

The Ventriloquist

He had been so lonely.
Days passed without the need to speak.
He understood at last
why God had made a man of the very dust.

It was a wooden woman
who came then into his arms.
He turned her face towards his own
and bid her speak.

She wasn't made precisely in his image
but she had charm.
Her eyes were skillfully painted
and she was sanded very smooth.

She could be dull, though,
and nothing she said ever surprised him.
Still, people smiled at them together.
He was definitely noticed.

Butter

Butter, like love,
seems common enough
yet has so many imitators.
I held a brick of it, heavy and cool,
and glimpsed what seemed like skin
beneath a corner of its wrap;
the dècolletage revealed
a most attractive fat!

And most refined.
Not milk, not cream,
not even *crème de la crème.*
It was a delicacy which assured me
that bliss follows agitation,
that even pasture daisies
through the alchemy of four stomachs
may grace a king's table.

We have a yellow bowl near the toaster
where summer's butter grows
soft and sentimental.
We love it better for its weeping,
its nostalgia for buckets and churns
and deep stone wells,
for the press of a wooden butter mold
shaped like a swollen heart.

Peaches

I have eaten peach after peach
without hesitation or apology, and each
was a disappointment. Outwardly
they looked ideal, smooth as a pony muzzle
or pool table felt, sunset colored,
and when I held them I sensed
either their heartbeats or my own.

I overbought, too, thinking how lovely
they looked together, a troupe of California peaches
visiting Minnesota in July, the only month
they'd find palatable. I wondered what exactly
I expected of them. Flavor, I suppose.

Or I thought the stone
might offer me I can't say what,
like tea leaves or a fortune cookie,
some hint of a changed life.
Still moist, still bearing a tassel of flesh,
the stone requests a sympathetic burial;
it believes that any amicable clay, even mine,
is suitable for resurrection.

Red Rover

What courage we had,
our infantry stretched across the yard,
no shields, no swords,
no cavalry assembled behind us
calming their nervous mounts.
We had the strength of our arms,
the speed of our legs.
We had our friends and our convictions.
Opposite us, the undulating line
of children drew suddenly straight.
It was early on a summer day
but the larks fell silent.
A high voice
invoked the name Red Rover;
we could not say who said it first.
But righteousness passed through us
like current through a wire.
Or like an inaugural sip of wine
burning in our chests,
something father gave us
over our mother's earnest
protestations.

Jump Rope

There is menace
in its relentless course, round and round,
describing an ellipsoid,
an airy prison in which a young girl
is incarcerated.

Whom will she marry? Whom will she love?
The rope, like a snake,
has the gift of divination,
yet reveals only a hint, a single initial.
But what if she never misses?

Is competence its own reward?
Will the rope never strike her ankle,
love's bite? The enders turn and turn,
two-handed as their arms tire,
their enchantments exhausted.

It hurts to watch her now,
flushed and scowling,
her will stronger than her limbs,
her braids lashing her shoulders
with each small success.

If Bees Could Vote

No doubt they'd vote en masse
like labor unions—or like gun enthusiasts:
for they carry concealed weapons
and would die rather than surrender them.
They'd vote like true conservatives
to keep every last thing they already have;
they'd vote stubbornly for their queen,
however rarely she travels the realm
or even shows herself. Most of all
they'd vote against the annual veil
of paralyzing smoke, the gray dream
during which half their goods vanish,
the vault door left wide open
in the pillager's haste.

Horses in Spring

Beware too much happiness!
The horses paused suspiciously before the open door,
snorting and stamping, while sunlight poured
onto the cold cement. They smelled snow
in the barn's shadow, mud along the south wall,
matted grass in the thawing pasture.
Their nostrils flared and their ears
lay back, then pricked forward, far forward,
and they stretched their elegant necks
as if the world were offering them a slice of sweet apple,
or something even more pure, on an open palm.

I was just a girl and couldn't understand
how they could hesitate at the edge of something
so intoxicating. Spring's first bee flew blindly
in then out again, all impulse, no plan.
At last with a clattering of hoofs
they left the barn for the bright paddock.

Even then they huddled together in their dull, thick coats,
superstitious, imagining a wrathful master
who would whip them for taking what is offered,
a master capricious as March.
I swung the heavy door closed
and climbed the fence to watch them,
the bay, the black, the pale appaloosa and the rest.

No one had ever broken my will, forced me
into the traces; I was too young for school.
They tested the earth with their sensitive hoofs
and didn't like it—too cold, too soft, too unpredictable.

Summer Night

The street lamp looks down;
it has dropped something
and spends the whole night
searching around its feet.
The rumble of a jet, and the fast road
blocks away, roaring like a cataract.
The scent of mown grass,
and of the body that mowed it.
The sidewalk, made of warm squares
heaved by maple roots,
covered with hieroglyphs in chalk.
A maple sapling, its trunk
wrapped to the knee
like the legs of a racehorse,
galloping straight up.
At dawn the prodigal sun returns
accompanied by equatorial birds
and a floral entourage.
What good has it done us to labor so
when all are rewarded?
Let the spade fall, then,
and join the feast.

Lemon

A lemon on the countertop
is a responsibility. Lemon-scented reveries
inspired its purchase; a modest investment,
yet one that now seems rash.

It was so plump, waxed and polished,
bumpers on both ends like a Volkswagen.
When I held it, it endeared itself to me;
I don't know how. A mystery of color,

as a flower draws the bee, bodily,
right down into it. Yet the lemon
was certainly retouched, like a photograph
signed love, Sunkist.

I scan the cookbooks, every recipe
beyond the likes of me. I think
of simply slicing it to flavor plain water.
At last I concede I'll end up doing nothing—

traveling, extensively perhaps,
to avoid the whole dilemma…coming home
to find the lemon hard and shrunken,
and bitter, quite impossibly bitter.

Poodles

They're out of fashion, I think, poodles,
like certain other accessories.
The puppy posed in a tea cup
or the topiary of a show dog, combed and quadripedicured—
unfathomable affectations.
Even their name is baby babble.

But poodles don't know they're ridiculous.
They think they're still dogs, the way people my age
still think they're sexy.
Indeed, an encounter between husky and poodle
supports the latter's conviction:
a quick sniff and the leashes do grow taut.

Dogs like this are our fault—all this toying with nature.
We drag a German cur, a hunter, a ratter,
indoors to a waiting lap, where its head
blooms like an elaborate iris,
and eventually, to be frank, it's a fop.

Yet on an idle day, after repulsing the mailman,
it discovers madam's open closet, and instinctively
sinks its teeth into the mink.

Peanuts

The shells are like modular houses
designed for families up to four,
meager and thin walled.
Economy is their sole recommendation.

But the nuts are rich and good,
individually wrapped in fine red paper.
Their light salt evokes the sea,
as if they'd roasted slowly on the beach.

The debris that remains after peanut consumption
resembles the rubble of demolition,
or the floor around the Christmas tree
after the irresistible excess of the season,

though we eat peanuts all summer, too,
driving here and there in a hot car.
They're full of the benign fat of populism:
a kind of People's Nut.

A Match

A match stands erect among its peers
like a prisoner or soldier,
smooth-headed and impassive
but secretly self-important:
eventually it will be selected
for a heroic but fatal mission
during which its expiration
may well mark the beginning
of a vast, unstoppable conflagration.
Whether for good or evil is no matter.

Somewhere in the hedge
a boy is playing with matches,
scorching twigs and leaves
and a passing beetle.
Finally he burns the empty book
with the last match
and on the count of three he awakes,
cross-legged in his smoky clothes.

The flame creeps backwards
down the stick, and soon
threatens the fingers.
Why is it we so often love
the worst thing for us?
Friction gives rise

to such ephemeral light.
Yet as it lingers,
doubled in a pair of dangerous eyes,
we finally meet our match.

Long Nights

"It's good to have poems that begin with tea and end with God."
—Robert Bly

A cup forgotten on the windowsill,
half full of cold tea, half of moonlight.
The rocking chair sits alone now,
its back erect and its seat ample.
There I nursed the first baby, and read
the *Alexandria Quartet*, wherein
a child was a further romance.
I still feel her in my arms, limp with sleep,
and see her heartbeat in her fontanel.
Whenever I tried to lay her in her crib
her eyes flew open. Let her cry, they said.
But I never let her cry.

My mother carried six of us,
one after the other, on her hip,
as we descended from her embrace
to our stations on the earth. She says
to this day her left hip is higher,
her left arm brutally strong,
her right infinitely dexterous.
Long were the nights she spent in labor
wrestling babies from the Creator.

Teeter-Totter

You were too shy to ask,
but she chose you as the Heavens chose her,
this bright, willing girl racing you
to the teeter-totter.
It's bliss to rise, to watch her close her eyes,
sigh and lean back,
her hair loose and long,
her legs parted by the thick green plank
that you share, while all around you
others swing back and forth, spin, climb and slide,
a carnival of motion that carries no one
beyond the sands of the playground.
Your feet touch the same earth
where countless others have begun and ended
their similar reveries, the world
in temporary sympathy with itself,
a great sea rising and falling softly at its edges.
And though you could never be tired enough to stop,
she wants to. So you dismount
as you began, as equals, face to face,
while others run to take your places
heedless and headlong.

The Lawyer

You dropped by after soccer practice,
the young athletes still sweating in the Suburban,
to collect the promised perennials:
shovels full of Siberian iris, sundrops,
the treasured Carpathian harebell.
You wrapped them in the *Wall Street Journal*,
your broad, flat hands pencil calloused,
the size of serving bowls.

More and more you look out the seventh floor window:
hillside and lake, traffic, scaffolding
for the Holiday Inn expansion,
and just outside the glass
a spider centered in its tremulous web,
a habitat rich with insects, but so exposed.
You spend your two hundred dollar an hour time
waiting for the sudden pigeon.

The clients are here about the will. Send them in…
Sit down. Sit down, please.
Such a beautiful day. How's the grandson?
The room, too, has aged: your framed credentials
no longer reassuring, the desktop a computer simulation,
the law library a collection of those hollow books
that fool thieves. Still the customary words draw near…
the IRS has narrowed the definition of…

in cases of incompetence…a witness to…should such action
prove necessary…At last a mental gust
blows the details into the lake
and the interview is amicably concluded.

The boys chased the soccer ball through the seedy dandelions,
all legs, like colts dressed in racing silks.
Odd how, after naming them, you hardly gave them a thought.
Not your department.
Once, coming home late from the cabin,
you almost hit a deer. Everyone woke when you swerved,
flung sideways, a burnt smell from the tires,
the black, indifferent trees directly in the headlights.
After that you felt both more and less adequate.

But nothing even wilted. Carpathian harebells
blooming the first year, sparsely, on frail stems,
sundrops spreading like pennies thrown at a parade.
Nowadays you're always puttering in the garden,
bareheaded, on your knees before the roses.

The Hypnotist

He began as a boy
by hypnotizing his dog and cat
through repetitive petting.
The same technique was less effective
later on girls; further refinement was essential.
He practiced on himself
using a mirror and a tape recorder,
but unfortunately it was
still his mother who eventually had to wake him.
His problem was he couldn't find
a suitable accomplice. The patient, he knew,
must willingly enter into the shadows,
enticed by the glint of his gold watch,
lulled by his voice.
She must be convinced that his power over her was
(and here he hoped he didn't flatter himself)
her best chance for a cure.

Two

Daisies

In the democracy of daisies
every blossom has one vote.
The question on the ballot is:
Does he love me?

If the answer's wrong I try another,
a little sorry about the petals
piling up around my shoes.

Bees are loose in the fields
where daisies wait and hope,
dreaming of the kiss of a proboscis.
We can't possibly understand

what makes us such fools.
I blame the June heat
and everything about him.

Postcard: Busy Clarence Town Harbor on a Mail Boat Day

Bahamas, 1962

The red truck idles,
dripping an unknown fluid into its shadow.
The sky is full of the sea,
of clouds that left the salt of their estate
behind in the rich water.
At night we feel the anchor drag, and the whole island
drift toward the southern cross.
But the morning mail boat finds the dock, and dark heads
bend over fluttering paper
as the inquisitive breeze reads over a dozen shoulders.

Love is everywhere, like the sand. Whatever is old
is still to be loved,
whatever rusts, whatever falls behind on the sandy road,
the oldest hen, the pencil stub,
is still to be cared for. At noon the mail boat, low in the water,
restarts its engines:
our last words must be weightless.

An April Walk with My Daughter

She asks, would you call this twilight or dusk?
It's the hour when darkness is as revealing as light,
so that Venus appears, and a thin, perfect
profile of the moon, trailing the sun like a pet.
The glass bowl of the sky is cleaner
than we could make it; the black of space
observes us through it—Earth,
like an aquarium, kinetic and self-contained.

When you were three or four
and we were working hard all day every day,
we came home to a cracked aquarium, remember?
A spontaneous rupture, ruinous water everywhere,
just an inch left for the danios, the neon tetras.
What became of their world, did they wonder?

In each puddle another false sky,
another black tangle of birch branches,
the spears of spruce tips, the echo of a robin
warbling after the worm feast.
Let's call it twilight that makes me
appear oddly younger and you older,
just as we each might wish.
The last snow was hard as a cast this morning,
but now it's soft, collapsing,
collecting in rivulets and coursing merrily away.

And the new tank pleased the fish.

It was as if God had moved them to a second planet,

fresh and temperate, free of blemish.

Honesty

I could easily be honest
if I were certain of the truth.
You remember the day as sunny and hot,
the car an oven, the air
rippling over the green chile fields.
I remember clouds building in the western sky
as quickly as if there'd been an explosion
out where the military tested
something big and vastly expensive
over and over.

Everyone seems so confident.
Those letters to the editor: "Get real" and
"Wake up, people!" The man from Pengilly
who keeps "loaded guns in readily accessible locations."

I honestly don't know why I had children
or why I sew, or garden,
except that if it's true we're made in God's image
we are born to create, or to try—
though when you smile at my earnestness
I see that you're right, I am naive.

I remember when our daughter realized
it was possible not to tell the truth.
She was three years old.

I saw something pass over her eyes, a petit mal,
leaving a kind of bright residue,
the shimmer of a most attractive lie, a fairy tale
no one had told her, yet she suddenly knew,
about a girl who never pinched a friend
however much she deserved it.

A hour passes and I'm no longer angry,
though it's true I was.
Sunlight streams through the screen door—
a late clearing, just as you predicted.
We're together in the kitchen,
a friendly bumping as we wash and slice
the green and red, yellow and white
ingredients, and stir them all in the kettle
until nothing is exclusively itself.

Black and White Photograph

She lined up the boys by height
and steadied her camera.
All were dressed alike, in nothing
but shorts and holey tennies,
nearly bald—their hair summer shorn—
and they fidgeted as she fixed them
in the tiny window, six boys,
ribby and scabby, their limbs aboriginal brown
under the hot Iowa sun
and thin as cornstalks.
Somewhere in the black camera
it is still 1956, and mothers are hanging
diapers on the clothesline,
a practiced eye on the clouds.
It seems in each life
a moment comes that the heart adheres to,
when light floods in to assemble
a single image in the dark.

Memorial Day at the Lake

The cousins drift far out in their inflatable raft,
but the water is calm, the sun generous,
Grandpa and Grandma are still alive, luck is with us.
A new hatch of children train to be sand-artisans
while aunts and mothers tan their winter legs.
Someone discovers a tick and hysteria erupts,
inspections, tears from the youngest—
"I don't want to be eaten!"

Around the campfire, a great circle of rosy knees
as the Family solves the Poland problem, restructures welfare
and deliberates the shortcomings of the absent sister-in-law.
The men still wear their feed caps in the darkness,
and moonlight falls on the brims.
The least wind makes the young aspens nervous—
they are so sensitive. They take things so seriously.
Shouldn't they be asleep by now?

Herd the kids to bed and come back to the fire,
the voices softer now but more frank, the beer cans light.
Someone says you can't be gentle
and still be a man. You put away childish things.
You lose a finger in the combine, it's gone.
And in the flames are other fires...the order comes
to advance, and it makes no sense to die so far from home,
to lift up your body to a bullet. Comrades fell,

but you came back to the floating world,
to buoyant days like red and white bobbers, sleepily tended,
to fields deep with sweet alfalfa.
The price of life is of course death,
but only one death, and so many lives.

It's the morning of speedboats
and water skis and excited novices.
When it's your turn to grasp the stick
and step onto the water,
to feel the pull of a hundred horses,
then think of yourself as a water beetle,
hard on the outside, light as cork.
Someone has lent you his life jacket
and buckled it snugly over your heart.
Everyone you love is in that boat, looking back.
It's far too late to say no.
These are your people.

The Midwife

She was a medium, a fortune teller,
or an emissary sent to God himself
to beg humbly that the child
come whole and sound
and soon. Her hands were so clean,
the nails clipped or bitten,
the skin dry and tight.
She slept off and on,
accustomed to resting when she could
in a bed or chair,
like a traveler crossing the frontier
between tragedy and comedy,
land forever claimed by both sides.
What she witnessed
was the opposite of drowning,
a reenactment of the moment
the first amphibian took a breath,
the tadpole of a child
swimming eagerly into her hands.

Woman Knitting

For Ann

Your hands, clean and nimble,
hover over a lap of wool.
They coax forward a single
tomato-colored strand,
which, during a brief ceremony
accompanied by tiny clicks
as of camera shutters,
forms a noose around the neck
of one aluminum wand.
Then your wrists tilt
and empty another drop
into the sea of the sweater.

A soft light falls over your work
which women admire
extravagantly, like a new baby;
which is afterwards ignored to flourish
under your care, yours alone.
It is a proprietorship
that knots one evening to the next
all winter.

The Exchange

Sometimes when I see a wad of money,
half an inch of twenties,
old bills, folded and straightened,
smelling of tobacco and palm grease,
I think of the cash my father showed me
when I was young, when we moved off the farm
and the ponies had to be sold, even mine.
The money was so small, so inert.
I think he wanted me to hold it,
to accept the diploma of adulthood.
A letter came later, a photo—my pony
with her first foal, brown and white,
a baffled look on its face. Neither of them
will have lived this long; the money, too,
passed by now through a thousand hands.

The Yearling

The yearling's back began to sway
from our riding her too soon.
The eldest girl had named her at her birth,
and had claimed her, as if she weren't fully born
until she was someone's property.
But it was I, light as a boy,
walking her in at dusk from her tether,
who first rode her.

Some things can't be done gradually.
Mother gave me a boost
and I wrapped my hand in her mane.
I felt her legs struggle to accommodate me.
I felt a cry go out through her whole body
as she swayed sideways.
Then she simply stood, bearing me,
as Mother stroked her neck.
We meant no harm.
We had no plan.
Everything about her seemed tender
that hour, as the sky turned pink,
then lavender, as she carried me
toward the looming barn.

We didn't mean to, but we used her
more and more. It was almost too late

when Mother said, "Enough!"
But her back did straighten.
She finished her growing in peace,
grazing that August beside the mare
who bore her, in the farthest pasture.

Wild Strawberries

I stopped along the road
to pick you a handful
of wild strawberries. They cost
only a mosquito bite.

Bearded with seeds
the berry has a long face,
a short life, and no house at all.
Yet, such sweetness—

Long ago, on the infant's cheek
appeared the birthmark
called strawberry. Of it
no trace remains.

Cloud after cloud;
at last a summer sun.
Still the strawberries
taste of rain.

A wild berry on the tongue—
Wake up!
One of its seeds is moving!

Raccoon

All raccoons are one raccoon,
private, cautious, clairvoyant.
How white its eyes are as it regards
my silhouette against the house lights.
Its body seems too powerful
for the delicate head and forepaws,
a creature both manly and womanly,
capable of force or seduction.

Each dusk we feel our human powers diminish.
I go back for the flashlight.
Its beam makes an amber wake across the grass;
feeling it, the lawn prepares itself for my feet.
The thimbleberries rustle—
It's there, the raccoon, in the labyrinth,
flattered by my curiosity.

All nights are one night,
unyielding, restless, absorbent.
I turn back to the yellow doorway.
Behind me, the raccoon steps forward.

Summer Yard

A raspberry, overripe, dangles
like a dress shoe hanging from a white toe.
It falls into the mulch
where scores of ants are waiting.
Underneath the garden lies heavy clay
dense as an encyclopedia
filled with discredited eighteenth century facts.
In such soil a corpse would never give up its scowl.

But the air, the air in late July!
Thank God I am alive to breathe it,
to take the scent of lilies
directly into my blood.
I can hardly sleep knowing it is summer
even at night, my windows open
to the conversation of maple leaves
that sounds so strangely like water flowing past.

And then all day I wonder if I'm dreaming,
so much green between two winters
that even the deer have grown persnickety.
One dawn I saw a doe and two fawns inspecting
crabapples. Not quite ready.
When I was a girl I thought of riding deer
like horses. I still believe
it would be possible for a child.

Children Near the Water

"Always there is much more happening than we can bear."
—Tomas Tranströmer

When we wake in the warm tent
the children are already playing near the water.
Their sleeping bags are like empty wombs
with silky red lining.
From here they might be anyone's children,
or the earth's, one dark, one fair,
one girl, one boy.
It's been a long generation in my family
since any of us drowned.
Back then it was father's brother Joe,
the most beloved son
whose body washed ashore
on the sands of Lake Michigan.
How strange it is that water is both
life and death to us.
I think of my father as a boy
holding his mother all night long as she wept.

The face of the water
changes under the moving sun.
How stiff I am after sleeping on the ground.
No life left in last night's fire,
just soft gray ash and two soiled
marshmallow sticks.

Dew shines on a strand of spider silk
that binds a tall pine to the earth
like a guy wire. I think I know
what it must have felt like
to be the spider,
dangling in a lake breeze on the fragile
filament drawn from its own belly.
The children hardly notice as I join them.
They're so fresh,
like spruce buds in May.
Their feet are still round instead of long,
like smooth paws. How calm the water is today,
just the smallest ripples
wandering at the whim of the wind,
as many going out as there are
coming in.

A Field of Barley

Wind passes over a field of barley.
Nothing could be more lyrical.
Why God favored Abel's burnt meat
I'll never understand.

Sometimes I imagine the hills of Nod
covered with barley, and Cain standing alone,
dark with sunburn, wondering
what more he must do to be forgiven.

Years ago I visited a blooming orchard
on the east slope of the mountains
watered by its own spring, and I thought
I'd surely found Eden.

At night we saw city lights glowing
far out in the plain,
but the dark rock rose behind the farm,
eternal and absolute.

Up there one could see tragedy
long before it arrived,
foreshadowed in the first act.
Dust swelled behind its four wheels.

Dread is our inheritance.
But what sprouts out of the earth
is our consolation, the good yellow grain,
heavy in our arms.

Checkers

Red was passion, black was strength.
Yet one checker always had gone missing,
a deserter discovered eventually
cowering under a chair cushion.
What was there to fear?
Only time itself would be killed.

I was one who never planned ahead,
who sent my infantry into any open field.
Under my command they aspired
merely to be captured,
jumped and hauled off, bearing the smiles
of the successfully defeated.

Who really wanted to be kinged?
To stagger under a crown
heavy as a headstone,
to wander the board without a court
or even the escort of a fool?
What was glory? I never understood the word.

Often some idle soul of a certain age
taught checkers to the young,
offering stratagems
continually overruled by blind luck.
Then came snacks and naps
and afterwards, the balance of the day.

So Like Her Father

"A glorious young bamboo has sprung up overnight!"

—Issa

My daughter sits cross-legged
on the tabletop and reads to me
as I wash the floor on my hands and knees.
Through an open door we smell the first lilacs.

In autumn she will leave this house.
I will never say the words
I remember from my father:
"When you return it will be as a visitor."

Still there exists a natural order
less compromising than our love, or hers,
or the love I bear my parents.

I scrub with water mixed with tears
and the footprints come away.
"I'm sorry," I say, "I wasn't listening."
She takes a sip of tea and begins again.

Boulder Lake

It was almost too windy,
but we steadied the canoe for each other
and took up our paddles.

The wind seemed to remember us.
It raised my hat brim to see my face;
it felt me all over.

May is always unseasonable.
The ice had melted in the tea-colored water
and the bugs were out early,

still whirling, lean as Sufis,
but subordinate to worldly impulses.
I once saw a mosquito

pickled in amber, a specimen
caught napping after its antediluvian blood meal.
How perfectly identical to

this morning's,
humming its traditional melody
then whining to be paid.

The island drifts toward us.
There we'll eat our long-stored apples
and rinse our sticky hands.

There we'll sit together
on our life jackets, your end of the canoe
still water borne.

We've been married
the way this island wed
its own isolation

centuries ago.
We float here, talking as always of the children,
nearly grown. Their fates.

It will be no different for them.
Their wake will disappear behind them
as ours has, maps useless,

celestial navigation
discredited. They too will approach
the threshold of the water

many times before they cross it.

Three

The Hammer

Here is an instrument as blunt
and hard-headed as its employer.
What has it done? It has forced the nail
waist deep into the wood,
while the nail has spoiled its pleasure
by bending. Now the hammer must
remove the nail with its huge teeth,
curved like goat horns.
The hammer must undo what is half done
and begin again with a new, willing nail,
a nail that seems guileless as it says, "I do."

Crude work is in the hammer's very nature.
No one wonders where it is to be grasped
with the whole hand. It's clearly designed
to strike, to crack a brown-haired coconut
or a marrow bone. It's a fist, only harder.
The hammer's simple tongue is easily acquired:
a few elementary ejaculations
and one is fluent.

Deep in autumn I sometimes hear
a distant, solitary hammer
drumming on shingles or a two by four
while falling leaves foreshadow
something whiter and more serious.

How soon our days end—
yet the manly hammer is the last to retire.
Its head grows cold, its eyesight poor.
Is that a nail, the shadow of a nail,
a thumbnail? We'll know in a moment.

Tag

You're no longer "he" or "she"
but "it," neutered by a shoulder tap.
Good friends see you and run away, laughing,
and you stand in the middle of the yard,
alone with the contagion of your fingertips.

Perhaps you are the goat upon whose head
the guilt of a whole culture is amassed.
Or this is your moment to conclude
that every man is an island.

You are cast out of the tribe, left to wander
the steppes, recounting your innocence
to legions of flies and worms.
Your only hope of redemption
is to doom another to the same fate.

And the dusk is full of the children's shrieks and cries
as they dart from place to place
like trout startled by a human shadow.

The Fugitive

How many years since I drove a long way alone
or did anything remotely spontaneous!
The ditches are full of last night's rain;
the old patched highway is empty.
Swamp stretches for miles,
drowned spruce, silver and black,
a few trees still alive on ground inches higher,
suffering the survivor's guilt.
Soon after I first beheld my daughter
I understood I was now a mother
until either she or I died.
And then we added a son.

My foot orders more gas and the car leaps up a rise.
Then the familiar sigh of descent.
Every thirty yards a sentry, a blackbird
bobbing on a cattail, scarlet insignia on its shoulder.
They trill as I pass, like English bobbies:
in each particular I fit the fugitive's description.
The car's shadow, attached at the wheels,
stretches with miraculous ease into the landscape.
Shadows are so limber, so young.
They're born every moment, painlessly, without a cry.

The faster the tires turn
the more they appear to be going backwards.

When the road bends, north is west.
I have childless friends with second houses
a thousand miles away, in some perfect place.
I have friends whose children are grown and gone,
but then there are the phone calls.

I slept beside her that first long year,
though the books say not to. The rules apply to everyone,
yet how different are our fates.
Most of us are born and die at night, I've read,
but I've grown to trust the darkness, the house locked,
everyone home from one urgent mission or another,
safe within the moat of the Milky Way.

Little Trout

The fish lay across his palm, quiet now,
lifting one small fin in surrender.
Across the water, drifts of mosquitoes,
the kiss of fish rising,
black spruce on the far shore
dead from the waist down.
Are you the loveliest thing, little trout,
that lacks self-consciousness?
Its mouth opened, then a sudden convulsion
and the trout flipped like a gymnast:
instantly gone, and the man called,
I was just about to let you go...

Ladder

It takes two to tangle with the ladder.
You seize one end, I the other: the ladder
both couples us and keeps us apart,
and we walk awkwardly, our thighs
banging on the rungs.

I suppose it's important
to clear the gutters before snow fills them.
You say it is. Perhaps you like
the climb, ascending the H's,
the titillation of the ladder's flection.

You like to see me this small, perhaps,
this worried. You like the sound
leaves make as you herd them along;
you like the pressure on your instep,
as of a stirrup, and the galloping wind.

Still it's a comedy prop, this ladder,
extending itself like an aluminum trombone.
I see us struggling, as amateur clowns do,
to establish a superior foolishness,
to make of near disaster a laughing matter.

Autumnal Tennis

for my daughter, Hannah

A cold fog lodges in the harbor,
but here on the hill the morning glitters.
The courts are vacant,
one net collapsed in a hard frost,
the lines obscured by maple leaves.
I recall summer's heat as from a previous life,
any lust for winning long gone, and the ball
that you give me and I give you
is like a wobbling child learning not to walk
but to fly—
      I see your breath and my own,
and from our torsos, too, wisps of vapor—
heat from the alembic of the chest
wherein body and soul are emulsified.
"I'm warm everywhere," you reply,
"except my fingertips…"
            with which you search
the fallen leaves for the third ball, the lost egg,
a remarkable egg to withstand such bounces and blows.
          Let it go—
for this is the last hour of tennis until spring.
Leaves skitter across the court on their fingernails,
each casting tomorrow's shadow. And I look away
as your serve passes through the low sun, and call,
"Good shot. Well done."

Half-Fallen Pine

All that kindly summer
I walked past the half-fallen pine
that had settled into the family's arms,
the invalid in the downstairs bedroom.
On one side its needles rusted
and dropped into the thimbleberries.
On the other sap rose, fresh buds formed,
and there were lucid days.

Where the danger was greatest
I stopped and looked up, past the pine,
at the patient sky. A squirrel,
light as straw, scrambled up
the camel-colored bark
as the pine tilted precariously
over its eventual grave.

So we fall part way.
The planet little notes this catastrophe
and the chickadees insist
we should cheer up, etc.
They flutter before me, busy as nurses,
asking, "How came you, in the first place,
to expect so much?"

I climb as the trail grows steep and narrow,

where summer's torrents have bared
the heads of rocks. Below me the pine half-lies,
surrounded by wild, anonymous greens
devouring the sun. The pine surrenders
all it ever possessed: a few square feet
and the light that falls there.

Hard Frost

The white alyssum lived as long as summer did.
Each time my shoe brushed the blooms, I smelled honey.

Now, as I uproot the annuals, I wonder if some part of them
might still be alive, the way hair is both alive and dead.

From blocks away come the sounds of demolition:
crowbar, saws-all, the boom of walls falling across a garden.

So late for such work. Today the lake is gray as cement
settled into its forms, beginning to harden.

Yet water is so compliant, so calm. It knows
that every path leads eventually to the sky.

Another sound in the still air—a dog locked in a garage,
barking through the hours, changing no one's mind.

Late September

The leaves grow lighter and lighter,
yet they fall. As the woods thin
a house becomes visible,
and a plume of smoke hand-feeding the wind.
There's no hurry if you don't care.
For thirty years nothing knew paint,
but the house still stands.
What is dust, that we should mark
if it fills our empty boots while we sleep?

Children love you at first the way a dog does.
But eventually they will reveal
the history of your offenses
in high voices that carry across the pond.
Day opens and closes like a camera shutter,
mechanically, with more haste than necessary.
The cat lays a chipmunk at the back step.
I think of its burrow, of all it hoarded,
and of nine consecutive lives without remorse.

New Snow

A layer of smooth new snow
is like a coat of fat on the earth.
But it's only water weight we've gained…
it's insulation…it protects the crocus bulbs,
white as ovaries. How can another storm matter
on land so very old? These are woods, not a park;
snow comes and goes without formalities.

The whole top of a pine snaps off,
but the tree lives on. Imagine a symphony
that circles back upon itself endlessly. Musicians
fail and are replaced. Instruments fail
and are replaced. New genius. New snow.
The winds, freshened by open water,
take up the melody…

It's good to see old tracks buried,
then make them again,
and yet again. We fell into this life without a plan,
the way snow pours out of a white sky
taking its shape from everything it finds.
We'll leave it the way
snow disappears in one warm night,
into the earth and into the air.

These Times

October, 2001

The wind labored all night.
Yesterday hundreds of yellow leaves
on the birches, today none, and the garden in ruins.
I shear off phlox and day lilies;
I pull out the cosmos and shake off the dirt,
a filthy mop of roots—but the blooms had such charm,
the laundered pink of aprons sewn in the 30s,
a shape so ideal it could serve
as the international symbol for flower.
For an hour it seemed we were not at war.
Then a shadow crossed the sundial.

Wind all night, and leaves on the run.
Panic and rumor up and down the street.
I watch television with the remote in my hand;
a touch of my finger
and a new bomb falls on a different channel.
The spores of violence survive for years
dormant in the soil; deep in a peat bog
a corpse is discovered, preserved for millennia,
having perished by strangulation.

Already snow has come to the Dakotas,
snow in Winnipeg, snow in Warroad.
It will start here tonight,
swirling among the stalled cars.

We're told to turn back our clocks at midnight,
to make a long night longer. Some day
I'll come across one I forgot, that tells the old time,
a watch in a drawer perhaps, a ticking oracle
with a face plain as a child's
that cannot hide what is wrong.

Grown Children

The full moon wakes the eldest son
on his makeshift cot in the living room.
You can sleep when you're dead, it says.
It's making good time across the sky
in spite of the wind,
like a car driving all night to cross the plains
ahead of the snow.

The grown children have returned in time
to say good-bye to their mother.
It's like Thanksgiving or Christmas,
cars parked on the lawn,
the little house so full. Early and late
lights are on; they feel guilty sleeping
or smiling or eating, rummaging
through her kitchen, observing
her needless frugality, cheese wrapped
in the lining of cereal boxes,
the freezer burning her day old breads.
Between hospital visits they rake and chop wood
and keep the bird feeder full.

Who feels it most?
Who puts the coffee on at 3 a.m.?
Soon there will be no parent to shield him.
The curtain will open

and he'll be standing at the picture window
where anyone or anything might see him,
his silhouette, holding his hot mug, waiting
for the inevitable celestial evidence
that day will come.

Heart Surgery

That day I sat astride the roof ridge
sorting cedar shingles and nailing them
in long rows, planting them, two nails each,
my hands sweating in their gloves.
Nearby the portable phone, silent and white,
napped through all this noise, like a good baby.
Or as if it were anesthetized
like my father, five hundred miles west,
whose afternoon was completely devoted
not to bridge or the Giants' game,
but to heart surgery,
to paying death a call, and coming away.

I moved across the roof as the sun
moved across the sky, and my apprehension
was as big as the house beneath me.
My job was to follow the blue chalk line,
east to west, carrying bundles of fragrant wood.
No one waited below, worried sick,
for word the house would live.
There was no hurry. It was November
and it never rains in Albuquerque in November.

Rush hour was beginning—I could see far off
where shining cars poured onto the freeway—
when the phone rang. Mother. It had gone well…

there were others to call…she'd glimpsed him
on the gurney as they returned him to his room,
"and I thought he was dead, he was so blue."
The sky all around me was blue,
but night would change that soon.
A cool wind rose from the valley, from the river,
and I shivered, looking west over the city,
toward Phoenix, beyond the mesa, across the desert.
I would see my father again.

Thanksgiving Day. I entered his room alone,
without husband or child, and took his hand.
Our hands were as alike as my left is to my right,
one a little larger, used to doing more.
The shades were drawn
but he showed me, in the dark,
where they'd parted his chest,
and it was a coarse, enormous, fresh scar,
like the first furrow on the virgin prairie.
It had been, he said, "tougher than I'd anticipated."

But his face was already
more alive than it had been for years,
the color back, the blood flowing
like a river undammed, whole and free
as it once was, flooding the brown valley
as it once did, and his brow was smooth
as he lay back against his pillow,
and said he was ready to see the children.

All Saints' Day

It happens that the world has run out of patience.
Sleet coats a smashed pumpkin,
and the wraith hanging in an immature maple

must be lowered, washed and dried, and spread
again across the child's bed.
A north wind strips the popple of its costume, and flagellates

its bare limbs. The hills wear coarse gray, for penance,
before they're cowled in white.
And all the candy energy abroad last night,

the candle flame that lit up a malicious grin,
the brass of car horns,
the pillowcases bulging with extorted chocolates—

All is surrendered. The soul is a cold cell in November,
with one supernal window
admitting a wan light accessible only to those

who have given up the ghost.

Christmas Fable

Each day we pour fresh water
into the Christmas tree's saucer.
It doesn't know it's dead—all this
care suddenly, these lights and jewels,
a tiara and a thousand earrings
after the modesty of the forest.

So the woodcutter's daughter marries the prince,
but this is hardly the end.
Wherever she walks she leaves a trail
of pine needles and the tack of sap.
Her voice is like restless water
below ice too thin to bear hunting dogs.

How can we tell if we are happy?
Beyond the window, pines sleep standing up,
like horses tied to posts
waiting since childhood.
We're too old now to go far,
but they're still waiting.

After Us

"I don't know if we're in the beginning or in the final stage."
—Tomas Tranströmer

Rain is falling through the roof.
And all that prospered under the sun,
the books that opened in the morning
and closed at night, and all day
turned their pages to the light;

the sketches of boats and strong forearms
and clever faces, and of fields
and barns, and of a bowl of eggs,
and lying across the piano
the silver stick of a flute; everything

invented and imagined,
everything whispered and sung,
all silenced by cold rain.

The sky is the color of gravestones.
The rain tastes like salt, and rises
in the streets like a ruinous tide.
We spoke of millions, of billions of years.
We talked and talked.

Then a drop of rain fell
into the sound hole of the guitar, another

onto the unmade bed. And after us,
the rain will cease or it will go on falling,
even upon itself.

Hartley Field

And place is always and only place
And what is actual is actual only for one time
And only for one place...

—T. S. Eliot

The wind cooled as it crossed the open pond
and drove little waves toward us,
brisk, purposeful waves
that vanished at our feet—such energy
thwarted by so little elevation.
The wind was endless, seamless,
old as the earth.
                    Insects came
to regard us with favor. I felt them alight,
felt their minute footfalls.
I was a challenge, an Everest...

And you, whom I have heard breathe all night,
sigh through the water of sleep
with vestigial gills...

A pair of dragonflies drifted past us, silent,
while higher up two bullet-shaped jets
dragged their roars behind them
on unbreakable chains. It seemed a pity
we'd given up the sky to them, but I understand so little.
Perhaps it was necessary.

All our years together—
and not just together. Surely by now
we have the same blood type, the same myopia.
Sometimes I think we're the same sex,
the one in the middle of man and woman,
born of both as every child is.

The waves came to us, one each heartbeat,
and lay themselves at our feet.
The swelling goes down.
The fever cools.
There, where the Hartleys grew lettuce eighty years ago
bear and beaver, fox and partridge
den and nest and hunt
and are hunted. I wish I had the means
to give all the north back to itself, to let the pines
rise in the hayfield and the lilacs go wild.
But then where would we live?

I wanted that hour with you all winter—
I thought of it while I worked,
before I slept and when I woke,
a time when the tangled would straighten,
when contrition would become benediction:
the positive hour, shining like mica.
At last the wind brought it to us across the pond,
then took it up again, every last minute.

About the Author

Connie Wanek was born in 1952 in Madison, Wisconsin. She lived on a farm outside Green Bay until the early 1960s when her family moved to Las Cruces, New Mexico in the Mesilla Valley. Since 1990 she has lived in Duluth, Minnesota with her husband and two children, where she works at the public library and restores old houses. Her first book, *Bonfire*, was published in 1997 by New Rivers Press after winning their New Voices competition. She has received fellowships and support from the Arrowhead Regional Arts Council and The Jerome Foundation, and won the 1998 Willow Poetry Prize.